Education
for the
New Millennium

Education for the New Millennium

By
Ann L. Atkinson, PhD

E-BookTime, LLC
Montgomery, Alabama

Education for the New Millennium

ISBN: 1-59824-369-1

First Edition
Published November 2006
E-BookTime, LLC
6598 Pumpkin Road
Montgomery, AL 36108
www.e-booktime.com

Acknowledgement

A special Thank You to my family and those students who decided to turn their grades and lives around for the better. You can make a difference.

PART I

Education for the New Millennium

Public vs. Private Education, has certainly been a subject, with much controversy, yet in either case, the question should include, what does my child feel most comfortable with, and in which situation, does my child best excel. Some students excel and do well in public school; others do much better in private and Christian schools. Yet more than the type of institution, does the student feel mentally challenged, and does the child feel accepted for who he or she is, within the walls of the facility? Students are bombarded by parental expectations, peer pressure, as well as their own expectations of themselves. So much of education, and past education, has found to be false, or just wrong, it has had to be rewritten, edited and added too, in order to correct misleading information that has been passed down from one generation to another, and as new facts are discovered, additional information must be added to the text books. What are your children learning in schools, when over half of the teachers must stop teaching their well organized according to the state Guideline lesson plan, to correct a child behavior or stop some name calling, or a fight about to beak out? Not because of poor classroom management, and students, who do and will not follow classroom rules. There is an under current of students who refuse to follow rules, who are disruptive, and do not respect parents, teachers or anyone else. The new agenda seems to be that it is cool to be a bad boy or girl, to get high, cut class, and get suspended or go to the youth center and or detention center. This does not usually occur in a private or religious school, mainly because parents pay tuition and if parents paid tuition for public school's there would be an improvement in behavior, and since public schools rarely have the best material or the top equipment, parents should pay on a sliding scale according to their income, and they should be held accountable for their children's behavior. Suspensions should be eliminated all together. If the child will not follow rules, take them out of school and send them to work doing manual labor based on their level of education, 8th grade dig ditches and wash dishes, 12th grade computer science, but programs that make them want to stay in school and want to learn. American's take their education for granted. They have forgotten how their forefathers fought to be able to read, especially African Americans. It is time for parents to stop being soft on behavior and learning. Out of 33 student's in a class only about four will go to a top university.

When a child is 4-5 years old the school system, has begun to test and make assessments as to whether they are on grade level if they can recognize colors, draw a line, and know how to say the sound of vowels and consonants by the 1, 2, and 3 grades. They are tested based on where they should be by their age and grade level, and when the student falls below that curve and has no abnormal physical or mental defects noted, the next step is testing for attention hyperactive or hypoactive disorder, or that the student just can't focus or be still for five minutes.

Well that is what they are suppose to be doing. Children 5-8 want to play, their attention is not designed to be drilled with math and English for 6-8 hours a day. Children in lower grades should have their attention on music, arts, physical education and then an hour or so on math, writing and reading. Changing the curriculum will make better students in the long run. By the time the students get to be 9-12 years of age they will be ready for intense studies of the upper grades. Children who learn social skills though interactive play have less behavior problems in upper grades. All children want to feel loved and accepted, and with all inclusive education children with physical as well as mental challenges are all lumped in the same class with an EC teacher to check on their progress. It is a good idea in theory but in the real classroom it can be a room full of disruption. A child that jumps up and down, runs around the room and hit's other students because they forgot or did not receive their medication and they are a level 4/5 504B student. Yet there is nothing that the teacher can do but take him or her to a quiet room for a few minutes, until the student calms down. Who has learned anything for that ten-minute interval? It is time for the educators to stop watering down the lesson to bring it down to a lower level, because students have been socially promoted, but it is time for students to bring their studying up to the grade level that they are supposed to be on. An 11th grader reading on a sixth grade level cannot pass 11th the grade chemistry. Yet this teacher is to somehow teach this material to a child with limited ability or take the time from the class and teach him to read, either after school or in a tutorial program.

Then there is a segment of students who are 18, 19, and 20 in the 10th and 11th grades who have failed prior grades. When students are being held back, somewhere in between going to that next year should be summer school and an additional program to provide make up and catch up work. This would eliminate people being 20-22 getting out of high school. Until we work together with love, respect and cooperation as a team, then and only then will change occur.

African American's throughout slavery fought for education and justice. Topeka Vs the Board of Education was the landmark case that made it possible for African Americans to have a decent education, as opposed to separate but equal. Mary Bethune Cookman started a college with $1.50 which made it possible for students to be educated in a time when there was very little for African Americans, in 1917. The NAACP marched with 15,000 people so that African Americans could be trained in the military as officers upon graduating from college. America has had some of the most prestigious black colleges and universities, and yet since the beginning of integration, African American students are going backwards instead of forward. White teachers cannot make black children feel accepted because they have no concept of being black, yet they can show love and respect and keep teaching, yet so often, you will hear a white teacher say, "What else can you expect of them? Look at where they live, look at their socio economic back ground." But it does not matter where you live, socio economic back ground, pick up the books, the library is free.

Free your mind and you will indeed be free. No one can take what in you brain and your knowledge away. Learning more and more will free you economically, mentally and spiritually reading and learning more of the variety of subjects makes you a well versed and well rounded individual. What kind of clothes you wear, will not get you accepted into anyone's university, neither will it get you the job that you are seeking, so who really cares what designer made the clothes on your back, and who cares if you have friends that are related to the greatest rap artist? That will not make you a star, and whether you wear gold, or drive a hoopde verses a Mercedes, it will not change reality until you have the education too support it. Students need to be trained for the reality that they want, while in school, so that they can live their dreams now as opposed to some day later, "When I get 45, I'll get around to becoming that nurse or engineer or doctor that I wanted to be when I was 17 or 18."

In Bergen County New Jersey, there is a high school, that teaches college bound classes for students that will leave high school and go straight to college, and there is also a program with vocational programs for students who will go directly to work, but these students, are trained for their vocation and licensed directly from high school. Whether it's LPN's, barbers, beauticians, dental assistants, office mangers, this school system has gotten to the core of the problems and made the students take responsibility for where they are going and what they want to be in their future.

There need's to be schools similar to this all over the United States. It would eliminate some poverty for students who are the providers, using illegal means. It would eliminate some crime which is in direct correlation to poverty. People are not stealing from stores because they just want to, most are poor and have little job skills. Waitresses and waiters make about $2.75 an hour and hope to make tips to make up the difference. In rural towns they do good to bring home 25.00 dollars a night, in larger cities, it's much different and they probably make much more, but, few people started out saying I want to do this job for the rest of my life this is my career choice.

When Thomas Jefferson, Alexander Hamilton and James Madison were gathered to sign the Declaration of Independence, it was not that they thought of the African American. A slave was considered chattel, a piece of property, and had no rights. A slave could be brought and sold for ten dollars. It was William Whipper, a businessman in 1837, who was freed by his master and spent thousands of dollars to free slaves and send them to Canada. It was then that he gave a speech to the Negro Intellectual Society about non-violence and how to be free from the oppressor, which was 100 years before Martin Luther King and Mahatma Gandhi. In 1839 Cinque, the son of an African slave, lead a revolt on the slave ship Amistad and refused to be a slave. He was captured, but eventually freed in Connecticut.

African American have been a race of proud people, they have been the first in accomplishing greatness. The first black Army General, Benjamin O. Davis, and later his son and the famous Tuskegee Airman. The first black Senator, Hiram Rhodes, first congressman Joseph Rainey from South Carolina on Dec. 12, 1870. It is ironic that both senator and congressman where from the Southern states, where it was prominent to have slavery, yet it was not the point of having slavery just for the sake of slavery. It was an economic growth period, cotton was king, and the South needed the slaves to keep their cotton picked and ready to be sold, the same with tobacco and other crops. It was the black man who was in the fields, which instituted another form of racism, the division among the race, dark skinned, high yellow and brown paper bag, and light bright and darn near white. All of this division stems from the field laborer and the house laborer, and the masses of master born bi racial children, that are not accepted by either race. There needs to be a clearing of consciousness in this country, a unity and diversity from the country to the city, that lifts up the young and the old. Then and only then can we be a nation at peace, a nation that produces children who are young and gifted; and black, Asian, Hispanic and white it does not matter their race, it matter's that they have character.

African American and Hispanic males are scoring 25% lower on test scores for college then all other groups. It certainly is not because of their skin color, it is because of the education that they receive. Until we change our curriculum to fit the needs of the child, not to where they are but where they should be and where they want to go, their reality trained for their dream's to be fulfilled in their now not ten years down the road. It can be done. It's up to Administrator and Board of Education to get to work and bring about change, and stop accepting the same status quo. Until you change something you get the same result. Some say why fix it it's not broke? Well, something is broke when the prisons are overcrowded with youth, and guns are infiltrated into the schools.

Why don't schools have psychologists on campus? Most families don't get along, so why would 1000 students going to school 180 days? There has to be more than a guidance counselor in schools, and it should not be their job to do testing but to look for troubled teens and get them the help they need before there is another school shooting. Administrators are so busy holding teachers accountable for class room management, keep those students quiet and on task, yet it is actually the quietest who will become your next mass murdered. Students need to take responsibility for their own behavior, and the consequences of their actions. Then what is the point of a teacher writing a student up and the principle does absolutely nothing. The psychosocial climate then becomes, we can do anything and the teacher really has no back up. Administrators who are not supportive of their staff leads to teacher turn over year after year.

The curriculum has long been associated with the aim of developing mind power. The intellectual power of memory and reasoning, regardless of subject matter, yet psychologists do not see that solving problems in math, or some other subject matter, affect solving real life problems that affect the life in reality of the individual. How is an A in algebra going to help me figure out how to pay my rent? Education must deal with real life issues that affect the growth and expectations of the person. How can you self actualize if you are surrounded by socio economic problems and there is no program to help you climb out of poverty? Education should be your ladder for success, not just in the four-year university, but also in high school, for students who are taking on adult responsibilities. Young mothers who have babies, with no job skills, who if are not dropping out they may well be on their way to doing so. Different kinds of education produce different affects on reasoning. A group of drug dealers on the corner have organizational skills, yet using these same skills in a positive format could run a small company.

In developing academic minds, three approaches are used, they are, basic operations, which includes classifications of things, generalization and deducing information, often more practical in science and the math courses that require exactness of facts. Yet with this approach and the next of problem solving as in word problems for mathematics, these do not assist in problem solving in real life actualities. The third is domain specific information, which is mainly used by experts in a particular field of study, yet this process would allow students to take apart what's known and come up with new ideas, using their own knowledge.

The emphasis on metacognition was used in the Cognitive Research Trust by Edward De Bono in his curriculum construction, however this does not go far enough. Like the scientific methods, there is much more to do in teaching children how to think, how to imagine their outcomes to resolving problems, that are useful in and out of the class room.

Herbert Wallberg has summarized the case for those who see American education falling far behind other countries in this global economy, which believe that there will be severe consequences on the United States being able to compete in the world markets. In the Soviet Union students take two years of calculus, and in Japan their students score higher on all tests than all other countries.

Vocational education has long been for students who go directly into the job market. Yet with new techniques and job requirements vocational schools will have to implement academics to keep up with the demand for jobs that require skills in computer programming or analyst positions. It is no longer the days of wood shops and industrial arts, much more needs to be done. There should be a system in place between technical school and the four year university, which will address the needs of the work force and the detailed training of the technical students, all of these issues need to be addressed in the area of preparing young adults for the work force. So where does the drop out, or the student who will just barely pass high school go? There are too many students sitting in technical schools waiting to get a G.E.D. because they have not had enough of the basics in high school.

Then there is the Alternative school setting, is it really working? There the student who cannot work in a large group, and there the juvenile delinquent, who has been sent from the courts, are put together. Those who want to learn, will, and those who want to turn their lives around do, but as a whole 29% drop out, go to jail, or get pregnant. The programs are there, but until the person makes the effort to realize they must change in order to fit into society, and that society is not going to change for them, then and only then will any program make a difference.

Society does not care if you sit at home all day and do nothing, but in order to become something, you must do something, create something, produce something, and be something. Someone who is a productive member of the society as a whole. If a man does not work, should he eat? If one is not mentally or physically disabled, or a child, who's responsibility is it to take care of a group of young, uneducated people that will flood the society in the next generation? Does this responsibility fall on the parents, the welfare, social services? Programs are changing to work first. No longer will one be able to keep having babies and doing nothing. So where will the underclass of people be? Living off those who have more. The have and the have-nots.

Society must take a serious look at all the institutions of learning as well as the affect of the criminal justice system. Poverty brings about crime. Eliminate poverty and you eliminate and lower the crime rate. No Child Left Behind will effect the elementary students, yet there is nothing in place for the students who need help the most, those who are currently suffering from low reading, math and science scores, those who have been socially promoted and labeled with Attention-Deficit and Disruptive Behavior Disorder, which most parents don't recognize until the school decides to test a disruptive student at about 9 years of age. These students usually have normal IQ's but may perform badly in school due to their inability to stay focused. And social personality disorder is also asssociated with ADHD when children have difficulty reading.

For ADHD to be diagnosed the criteria should include inattention, hyperactivity and impulsive behavior. Because some children live in an environment that is chaotic, and they mimic these systems, ADHD should only be diagnosed in children who live-in a normal socially stable home environment. The child being placed in a different environment may thrive and excel, when moved away from the chaos. Therefore nature vs. nurture comes very much into play. Students who break rules, lie, steal, and are classified by psychologists as conduct disorders that usually happen around adolescents, when the teens are trying to find themselves or identify with their peers, when they want to rebel against authority. Boys stealing cars for a joy ride, bullying other students, yet all these behaviors cause harm to themselves and others. Courts close juvenile records to protect teens, yet today teens are committing crimes that carry adult sentencing. Preventing these problems begins with the parents, the schools and society as a whole. It does take a village to raise a child, but it also takes a community that cares for one child at a time.

Children who are separated from their parents often suffer from separation anxiety disorder and have trouble adjusting to a new caretaker. Children who face trauma often stop speaking and may refuse to speak in a school setting, which is often selective mutism.

Another problem that affects children is being in foster care. Being taken from the biological parent and later moved from one foster home to another which causes a stereotypic movement disorder. These children tend to do body rocking, biting and hitting.

Educators have to take all of these behaviors into consideration. Sometimes, they have been informed from past school records, and reports from psychologist and therapist, other times, they have little or no information until the student has been assessed and evaluated. Often the evaluation is done by a team of teachers, counselors, social workers and psychologists. After several weeks of testing it will then be determined the appropriate learning level for the student. Usually students outgrow these behavior problems as their home environment changes for the better.

Educators by law must report any kind of physical or sexual abuse reported to them by a student, regardless of who the perpetrator was.

With all the factors that influence education, it is a wonder that a classroom can be conducive to learning. Yet the teacher must make the classroom a safe heaven for the students, and a climate that allows learning to take place.

Administrators and teachers have been taught how to do just that, by posting classroom rules and the consequences for not obeying them. Effective teacher training requires parents to be involved in every aspect of their child's learning, and each child should have a plan of action that they are responsible for. Teacher are to always deal with the behavior without injuring the self worth of the child and allow the child to take part in problem solving, responsibility and self-discipline. This may work for high school children, but not for middle and elementary students.

Rewards for students who behave and turn in assignments on time. The teacher has positive expectations that the students for the most part will follow the rules. But when students do not follow the rules students who fail to follow procedure and routines cause it. Students learn when they are actively involved. Classroom procedures are followed daily and the students know automatically what they are supposed to do when they walk in the room. Effective teachers start with the beginning of the school year, explain, rehearse, remind and experience these procedures, so when Christmas break is over and students forget, they are reminded and the procedure is reinforced, it becomes almost like a habit. For students who have behavior problems this is repeated over and over until they will conform or be excluded.

As educators and school counselors do more for students, they advance to their full potential. Then will we see dramatic change and growth in these students, self-confidence and improved academic scores. It is not enough for schools to receive State and Federal funding, it is more important that the people who run these schools care and teach these students with enthusiasm as well as offer the support, so one child may say, "Ms_____ or Mr._____

when I was in your class I admired your ability to make me think, to make me feel good about myself. You were my role model."

As for teachers who get involved with students in a sexual or abusive relationship, they should be fired immediately and never teach anywhere. Students who don't want to learn, it is usually because of something, they don't know and are afraid to ask, for fear that other students will make fun of them. Teacher's who recognize this are able to help students on an individualized basis. If a child feels loved, respected and that his ideas are important will, most of the time, be challenged to do more. Children must have a clear code of ethics that must be followed; this will make public schools better across the country from the city to the country.

Educators can no longer applaud bad behavior or look the other way. Suspension is useless. Send a child home to watch TV? Because parents are at work, the best solution is in school or after school suspension, or a schoolwork project like k. p. or yard duty. Sometimes educators make excuses by saying this child came from a broken home or this child's mother is on drugs. This is no excuse for bad behavior. Society does not care about what you went through. When you go to work they just want you on the job working. You can't go to work and say, my parents got a divorce so I can't work today. When educators require higher standards from students then the students will reach those higher standards.

It is important that schools provide social graces as well as math and science, English and social studies. Children have lost their innocence and need to go back to play and physical education before the core subjects. Parents need to be more cognitive of the hours that their children watch television and it should be limited to their age group as well as what they are watching. Americans tend to be consumers rather than producers. With proper training and education, the next generation will be the inventors who make products with made in America stamped on them. Allow students to be creative and to enjoy learning by participating in their own curriculum, so that all the new energy in their thought can become a reality of a new product or a new service which will benefit mankind. These students will invent new forms of energy from heat to electromagnetic light. These students will invent new ways of travel, and new modes of communicating. All of these things are in the future. There are no limits to what the mind can conceive and invent if the future students will believe that they can achieve greatness, it is within their reach. It is time for teachers to stop saying I've got mine and you've got yours to get, but to get themselves on the bandwagon and bring out the best in each child that comes into their class room. We must lift our minds, our heart and our hands to our children. These children will make the world a better place. These students must be taught today the reality to make their dreams come true tomorrow. These student are our genius, we need only to open the door way to their mind and hearts.

Children, who misbehave do so usually out of lack of love and attention from home. They will seek it from peers, lovers, gangs, drugs, and anywhere else that they feel they are accepted and a part of a group. It is the parents responsibility to make sure that their children know that they are loved and safe. To many parents are too busy working overtime, time and a half, and comp time to realize the effect that not spending enough time with them will eventually have on the child. Often children have to take on adult responsibilities at an early age and it should not be so. A ten year old should not be taking care of the younger sister and brothers, and cooking dinner or fixing sandwiches until somebody that is an adult gets home. Latch key kids shouldn't be home alone, not even for a minute. If someone breaks into the house and takes the child, what are you going to say, "I was at work?" It's time for mothers to step up and be mothers. Either work while the children are in school or get a day care, after school care provider. Nothing is more precious than your children. Allow a child to be just that. When they are old enough to take on more responsibility then give it to them, but allow them to be children.

Television, has already allowed them to grow up too fast. Restrict the hours that they watch TV and they types of programs that they watch. The brain has powerful input for things seen and heard from all kinds of things; children should not be exposed to everything. Thoughts are like mighty sound waves traveling through space, eventually they take form. As a man thinks, so is he. The quiet child who sits in the corner never talks, but goes outside and kill's the cat, is tired of mama putting him down, and saying you are just like your no good daddy, will be the same child who ends up on TV for a major crime or in a mental institution.

We need parents who walk and talk positive to their children and to each other. It is time to end the negativity in the family. The family is the foundation of society, it is the glue that holds the communities together. Communities need to reach out and help their neighbors, and if each person would take the time to help the one just next door to them, there would be no more homelessness in this country. We can no longer sit around and say that's the Governments problem or this person is on welfare, if you got more than someone else give it away, you can't use it all and you sure can't take none of it with you. The hearse never pulls up with your favorite chair, TV, car or house. It's time for America to slim down not just in weight, but in being greedy and materialistic. Get rid of some of the stuff and give it to the ones less fortunate than you. For all the millionaires, go down to the projects and build some houses that the people can own and that they can be proud to keep up. Charge them 250.00 dollars a month and in ten years let them own them. Forget a thirty year mortgage.

If you make things affordable, yet of good quality, the whole economy would be better. We have products made in China, made in Japan. When are we as Americans going to stop outsourcing our jobs and start making quality merchandise right here? You can't tell a company that you should not move overseas because they would rather pay 1.00 a day for labor as opposed to 6.00 an hour. But by the time you ship the product back to the States and pay taxes on it have you really saved that much? Where is the pride in being an American and helping to build up the economy of your own country? Perhaps the small businessman with the candy shop needs to come back to the corner of every neighborhood; at least he can give the boy that is standing on the corner a job. So most of us say, "I got mine the hard way, I worked my way through school and started my business with less than 1000 dollars, look at where I am today." But somehow, you surely forgot that someone gave you that inspiration, some old school teacher made you aspire to do great things, some neighbor down the street made a difference.

We are all in this global market together. If there's a water shortage in Japan, before long it will be in the US, the streams keep flowing, rivers keep rolling, they all flow from the same ocean sooner or later. Just like the rain comes down it'll go back up in the form of evaporation. Everything goes around, even mankind, to the dust it return and shortly after one family member exits life's stage, then a new family member is being born somewhere. The universe supplies enough of everything for everyone, only we must learn how to be good stewards over what we have and not be afraid to give it a away, to share with the rest of us who have less, because if it continues to be a capitalist, selfish society, the folks on the bottom will revolt to get to the top. A trickle down effect makes a difference. If the President says give everyone in your company a 10% percent raise from the top to the bottom, watch product and sales go up an additional 50%. Don't believe it? Try it for 30 days.

Most important of all is to love yourselves and your children, have faith in your higher power and know that the children are the future. Allow them to live their dreams and make their mark. You live your own dreams, you can't go back you can only go forward. Set the example of what a role model, loving parents should be, and give to those who have less, so that your revolving miracle continues to flow, like air circling around the globe. What you give comes right back sooner or later. Make a difference in a child's world and stand for moral righteousness. Raising our standards and raising our level of consciousness will make the schools, the parks, the communities and society a united and better place for each of us. We can no longer say that problems belong to someone else. We all must pitch in just like keeping the paper picked up, we all must do our part to stop liter and pollution. We all must lend a hand and help one another up, it does not matter who's child, what race, we are all one people, one nation. We all must pull one another up. We've held each other down too long in the name of education, in the name of affluence, it's time that we look back and go back, and pull up and help the sister, the brother, the mother, that somebody left in that nursing home because they didn't want to remember she scrubbed floors to send you to school, or that sister who did without so you could become the big executive director that you are today. We all owe somebody, it's time to pay up. And if you are too proud to go back and say you're sorry and do something for them, go back to that place you came from and help two more children. Give some scholarships to the best schools, too some struggling child that everybody said wouldn't be nobody, because nobody took the time to believe in him or her. You too can make a difference. One person at a time will make one village at a time become a great and prosperous, productive nation.

It is amazing that we have public schools at all. Look at all the social issues that the school must face. Does the child have proper nutrition? If not free lunch, can they afford lunch or not, if not free lunch. Is the child being neglected or abused? If so there's a plan in place for social workers, counselors and individualized learning plan. The child is placed on an IEP based on his mental or physical disability, and in cases of ability to learn depending on the test scores and his cognitive and reasoning ability. Yet, these should not only be assessed by school psychologist but by a psychologist that specializes in disorders of the brain, even a neurologist. Just because there is a learning disorder this child could very well be learning based on the material that he is exposed to picking and choosing what he wants to learn. You can take that same child, put him in front of a computer game or let him listen to a rap song, or

Britney Spears, and that same child will know every move on the game and win, as well as every verse in the song. Children tend to learn what they are interested in. Teachers need to teach from where they are, if math is the subject let them rhyme and rap that math, repetitiously until they know it.

The methods of teaching needs to fit the modern student, who are selective in what they choose to learn. You can set a child in front of a television program, any cartoon, a three year old can tell you every character and what part they play in the story. My grandchild 3 years old can tell me everything on Clifford the Big Red Dog and Zoboomafoo, and know the animal and what they like. But although this is an exceptional child, children who are read to daily and in school early, as well as transition with smart start into pre-k and kindergarten already have developed social skills, and know words and vowel sounds.

Yet home schooling may work well if the parents are well rounded and academically inclined. The only draw back is that it does not allow the child to be socially well rounded. The interaction with large groups of other children is lost, and as an adult this child may well feel isolated and or less confident in a large setting, when going into college etc. Children who lived very sheltered lives, when they leave home and go away to college and or the military, tend to just run wild, drink a lot, get into trouble, and party like they have never been anywhere. They act almost as if their childhood has been a place of confinement for 18 years. Parents need to set limits, but at the same time know when to allow those young adults to be independent enough to make responsible decisions. When my daughter was sixteen, she thought I was the worst mom in town because other kids could hang out until 2am and go to the dance and skate clubs, but she had to be in her room studying, complete the assigned homework and then move on to outlining the next two chapters. Just in case you get sick one day, you'd already be ahead, that was my motto. She resented that, but it was for her own good. She graduated the school valedictorian and went on to college and graduated with honors. Now I call and say, "You going out?" She is staying home or working on some big project. Now she doesn't want to hang out. It's amazing how things change. We all have adversities in life, but when parents have children who are 16, 17, 18, 19 and still at home, with no job, failing school and having parties at home, or having a house full of their friends over, which is the parents?

If you're not trying to do well in school, get your GED and go to work and move out. When are parents going to stop taking care of children who are telling the parents what to do? Somehow the roles of parent and child are being reversed. The children are having their way and you hear parents say it's because of the laws and you can't spank them anymore. Well, when the child can't follow rules and is refusing to follow your plan for your household it's time for that child to move out, to juvenile detentions or someplace else. Every household has to have a structure and order for it to stand.

Actually it's two parents who work and pay the bills, and the sad part is that the economy requires two incomes to live a life of affluence, but some how the children are losing out with two people working. Women's liberation was not designed for working mother's, it was designed for wealthy women who didn't work in the first place, and it certainly was not designed for women of color, because women of color always worked. They were the ones who worked to take care of the other women's children and were their maids and nannies. So African American women have always been liberated and acclimated to work and the work ethic. It was the grand mothers who worked for rich white families and often brought those hand me down clothes home for their children, these were the same women who took in ironing in the fifties for 50 cents a week. African American women where the ones who often raised the children by themselves and they did not tolerate bad behavior period, but of course you knew better, it only took a look, and you knew to behave. You knew the meaning of God and family and the community, and it was also the neighbor's responsibility to look out for you. If Ms. A saw you down the street, she would bring you home and tell your parents. She had the authority to chastise you too. You were not spanked but you got a good talking too about what was expected of your behavior. Societies expectations of young adults have changed. If you expect great behavior good manners and excellence in young adults they usually, most of the time, will rise to the occasion. All teachers, administrators and adults should therefore expect and receive the best and when they don't, ask why not?

It is disturbing that about one fourth of our African American males are dropping out of school, heading towards incarceration, because some one has convinced them that it is alright to be in trouble, skip school and commit crimes, not realizing that the choices that you make as a teen will affect the rest of your life. If you steal a car at 18, that same crime will be on your record when you get fifty and want that job that you finally got your degree in and won't be able to get it because of your record. No child left behind can't help these students. They are already two are three grade behind. Neither does alternative schooling. Alternative schooling is a step between getting your act together and returning to regular school or your next step is jail. There should be some school program in place just for catching up, but even in the technical schools that offer G.E.D. programs, drop out end up there two or three years because they are placed there to learn on their own. If they didn't get it with a teacher teaching the material how are they going to get it sitting in a learning lab learning on their own? The theory makes sense to have the learning lab, but the learning lab serves no purpose if it does not teach from where the student left off and promote them to move forward, in order to get job skills or go on to a university, it serves no purpose. Like a cafeteria that serves only vegetables, and you have a group of people who want meat.

In test after test the results continue to show that African American males are far behind the rest of the culture. When children continue to be tested year after year to determine if they are where they should be it tends to make them lose interest in school and there should also be other ways of assessment by these standardized testing moguls. Teachers often use in class work and labs, or hands on experiments. Something else should also be in place beside the end of grade testing.

Some students have gifts that they do well in various activities. Boys tend to do well in building circuits, and parallel series in science or dissecting frogs, but may make only a C on the test, but they can tell you exactly how those wires work.

According to Erickson stages of development, in the stage of Latency about 6-12 years of age students are productive, socialized and well able to be competent in intellect subjects, yet at around adolescence, they become self-centered and ego driven, where they are most often influenced by their peers or a role model. Since we know that this is a transition into adulthood where the individual is trying to find their purpose in life, it is more important for adults to play major roles as big brothers and sisters, especially for adults who have accomplished much to be a positive role model in their lives.

According to Kohlberg there are stages of moral development and at stage three or level 3 there is the post conventional morality from adolescence to adulthood, that the individual wants to maintain the respect of their equals and the social order, as well as follow laws and order.

Freud's psychosocial development in the last stage, show that sexual development is the primary focus, which begins at age 12-adulthood. Yet Freud's suggestion of a conflict with sexual orientation, begins at ages 3-6 when they identify with the same sex parent, and may have a conflict either Oedipus/Electra complex, but it is up to the parent to set the boundaries. It is not normal for the daughter to be in love and have a sexual relation ship with the father nor the son, with his mother. When this occurs it is sexual abuse and it must be reported. The child must be removed from the home and the offender as well.

Child abuse can be physical, sexual, psychological and emotional. All of these problems show up in the classroom. When a six year old is talking about sexual things it is not age appropriate, and an 11 year old has body changes of a sixteen year old size 36B and big hips, who was just a few months ago a size three, there are clear indications that something is amiss. Children will act out, run away from home, and often tell a school friend and or teacher of this abuse. When told of this, immediate action must be taken. It must be reported to the Administrator and then to child protective services. The same with physical abuse, the child comes to school, with marks, burns etc.

Yet most of the time the abused child is quiet and acts normally, until it has become apparent to anyone and it all spills out. Children who constantly act out and have anger issues are often being abused at home.

The school system takes care of your children for 7-8 hours per day; whatever is going on at home will eventually spill over into the teacher's lap. Younger children will tell everything, that goes on in your house. Look at this scenario. Two boys talking, they are both 6 years old. "My mama didn't have no money so our lights got cut off." "Well," the other boy said, "why don't she have no job?" "Cause she's smoking that rock." "Well," said the other boy, "ask your mama if you can come to my house, we got lights." "O.K." said the other boy, "I don't have to ask, and she won't be home anyway." Now does the teacher ignore this or call the parent in for a conference to see if there is some program available to help them? This is not the teacher's responsibility, yet it affects why Johnny didn't do his homework.

In rural counties, schools require teacher's to do Home Visits, and often once they are done things change for that child at school, but they are very rarely done by teachers anymore. In a generation of do your own thing, disrespect is the norm. It is time for a change in the way that education is viewed. It is time for education to fit the group of students it is trying to teach. Of course we know that students are tracked based on their test score, and that there are multi level classes, but more than having your talented and gifted students on the college bound curriculum, and the other students on a general course of study, students should be choosing classes that they are interested in to prepare them for what they want to do. All students just aren't going to college. Some of them will take up a trade. Find out what trade they want and prepare them for it. Education has to change in order for it to be effective. It can't be a place where children are being warehoused all day, and some who want to learn will, and others are just sitting there doing nothing and refuse to do any work. High school students, sitting in class, and making zeros every day, because they don't feel like doing any work, and nobody at home is going to care or require them to produce anything. Yet this attitude does not prepare them for society. When you are a 20-year-old droop out what kind of job can you get? Even McDonalds wants you to have a diploma or G.E.D., if you can't count, the business is going to lose money.

It is sad to think that our schools are not doing all that they can do. With limited state funding, and Teacher Certification Requirements, under no child left behind, a lot of good teacher's are leaving. If you are a new teacher with two classes left for Certification and no money to pay for them, your job is over. Every program has to be funded. And forget Music and Art, most of those programs are cut completely. Children need to be exposed to all the cultural events, and they need the field trips; yet how many candy sales, can you have a year? If schools were independent and self supporting that would make a difference, but they are not and there is a class difference. If the same public school student could have the same education as the top private school, and or boarding school curriculum, it would make a difference. Children in inner cities don't go to fancy banquets and dinners. They don't go to places where they have a cotillion Ball, they are just trying to survive. To keep somebody from shooting them on the way to school and a 7th grader is telling the teacher, "Forget you, I make more money than you selling dope." All of these issues are social issues. Law enforcement must do something to keep the children safe, and so does the community. We need more neighborhood watch. We need to take our streets back so that they are safe to walk down, and father's need to stand up and be that, fathers. Men having babies and talking about their baby mama drama. But they are not paying child support or taking up the time with the child, and even more scary, it's the teenage girls getting pregnant and baby's daddy is in jail and she thinks that is great. There are enough young black males incarcerated to start a whole city, and these same children come back to school and say, "My daddy in jail."

Then you have Administrators who say, well this child, started a fire from smoking in the bathroom. I'll dismiss it this time, because he comes from a broken home, the next time he'll burn the building down.

Teachers have been limited by Administrators in reported offenses by students, because often the referrals are dismissed, and if you send down too many you must have classroom management problems, or if you have to many F's at report card time, you must not be teaching the material. When are Administrators going to require that the students be held accountable for their own grade and their behavior? Sure we know teachers who if the students had worked hard and is a borderline 65 student but does not keep disruptions going on in the class, will add another 5 point for class participation and being on time to give that child a 70 to pass a D and on the other hand that child who is disruptive with that same 65, who never does anything will get an F, so no one can tell me that behavior, manner and respect doesn't matter, it does, and that will take you just as far as having academic knowledge. Most people get jobs because of a referral from somebody who already works there that knows somebody else, and at other times, they are already filled from somewhere within, another department or whatever.

When students say you gave me a C, I used to say, you gave yourself a C, you make your own grades. Just like putting money in the bank, if you don't make a deposit you can't make a withdrawal. This generation of "your suppose to give me something, just because I'm here" has stemmed from the parents who give thier children stuff without requiring them to do anything, no chores or yard work. The student must earn something on his or her own. When a child does the work and makes that A, they begin to feel pride in themselves and they raise their confidence level and their self esteem and it makes the teacher feel satisfied that they have done their part. Students being able to explain and give the information back to her, not from memory but actually knowing the material, that's what teaching is all about. Schools need social workers on campus. They need psychologists on campus, they need additional guidance counselors and truant officers. There has to be a change in the public school system in order for it to do what it is designed to do. There are too many social issues that the child has to bring to school and with a large school, it will eventually lead to chaos if there aren't changes made. Police on campus and a metal detector does little if the student makes a bomb in the science lab or deadly virus in the Biology lab.

With drug abuse, and crack born children this all inclusive class room does not work and no matter what the law says, some students need to be put in a separate class room, and Special Education is not always the answer. A child addicted to drugs may be an A student then the next minute he is screaming his head off, taking about things on him. You call the parent and they can't leave work until a couple of hours. What does the Administrator do, sit them in the office until the parent comes, and they get worse because the attention warrants them to continue the inappropriate behavior? These students often go from passive to aggressive behavior within seconds. Having false conversation that have no reality to them that may borderline paranoid problems.

All of this is the responsibility of the school and when the police are called, it's taken to yet another level that involves the court system.

In order for the public schools to be effective, we must make changes, and most of the changes lay on the parents, parents that are loving, respectful and give their children the tools necessary to become responsible adults. It does take a village, a community and a group of professionals to raise a child into today's society, but even so we must give our best and expect the best from the children. They are the future leaders, the world will be their oyster, but only with kid gloves should we discipline, and even then show love and the reason for the grounding, or removal of a privilege. We have within us in this day and time, the ability to take charge and make changes, but it begins with one teacher and one Administrator at a time. We can do this. We owe it to our children, the same way that our parents sacrificed for us to be where we are today.

Behavior modification is not as easy as it sounds. The classroom environment is set up for learning to include bulletin boards that reflect the theme of the subject being taught, classroom rules, and motivational themes. However the way that a student acts, depends largely on several factors, to include what they bring from home, and the environment, as well as their emotional and physical maturity.

According to psychologists Piaget, Skinner and Maslow, each child must pass through various stages of development and, as they progress they mature, being capable of perceiving their world and their physical being. "In the age of MTV, suspension is a treat. I will not send students home to watch television," quote by Principal of T.C. Williams High School. "The students who spray painted the parking lot will pay for the damage."

Behavior is learned internally and it cannot be touched or seen. Psychologists measure behavior by scoring evidence of change over a period of time. Children learn from modeling their parents, siblings, and their peers, depending primarily on who has the most influence. According to Maslow, as each need is met, the child reach's Self-actualization, but according to Piaget their behavior is based upon growth, maturity, and the environment, as well as intelligence. Learning behavior is based upon response and stimulus in the form of classical and operant conditioning as reported by Dr. B.F. Skinner.

Classical Conditioning reflex is a response that suggests a physical or emotional response to stimulus, based on the situation and the response will result in a physical reaction or an attitude as opposed to learning something new or learning how to react in a different way.

In Operant conditioning the response and stimulus is based upon a system of reward and punishment or positive and negative reinforcement. Rewards programs for good work or applied effort. Positive reinforcement is used to get the desired behavior to continue, negative reinforcement is used to get the undesirable behavior to stop, such as having the time out area in the classroom. Teachers use the time out; call parents, and conference with team leader and parents, along with detention to try to curb negative behavior. Yet the problem is not with the schools alone, it goes much farther and deeper into the mainstream of society as a whole. According to psychosocial studies by Vineland, parents who use corporal punishment and withdraw their love for misbehaving children are increasing the potential for their children to become aggressive, and anti social in society.

Classroom instruction must take place in an environment geared towards learning and not correcting problems of behavior. In the classroom with 25-30 students six classes per day and 150-180 students with 25 percent having behavioral problems, there is something truly ailing society, and it is being reflected in the school system.

Accordingly, the nature of positive and negative reinforcement does not work if the student gets no gratification for what the stimulus or response is. In order for it to work at all it must meet the law of cause and effect. I will behave if my grades are jeopardized. However for the student who does not care about his grades or detention behavior modification does not work in a normal school setting. The scales of behavior implemented by Piaget and Vineland indicate that children should develop mentally, physically, and intellually at the same time, in order to change their behavior, that their behavior changes as they mature and become more precognitive of their surrounding and themselves.

A 1980 study done by the Census Bureau of 3,000 school children age 3-12 indicated that the children lacked in communication skills, in behavior skills and emotional maturity for their age group. That some students were maladaptive to society.

In a study by Sears, 1953, he concluded that adolescent males were more likely than females to have been beaten in the homes, and were more likely to end up becoming abusive to their spouses and or in abusive relationships. According to sociologist on shoplifting, ages of criminal shoplifters are white males 11-17 and that if their behavior is not challenged; they are more than likely to become involved in an adult crime. Those students tend to conform to society if it is within their group or subculture. That class and status has a great deal of influence on behavior, that students in an affluent neighborhood, may go to the private school and only associate with the most affluent, that students who are in the poor urban setting, will attract an element that is geared towards drugs, crime and etc. However there are cases such as Dr. Ben Carson who grew up in the projects and became a physician. Conforming to class room rules reflects conforming to rules set at home; however there are cases where children have no rules set, parents are not at home, children are homeless, and latch-key children are making their own rules. In order to change behavior children must fear the consequences for the misbehavior. Secondly, reintegrating shaming, negative behavior is not used in the school system, because it is considered a put down or lowering the child's self-esteem.

Research finds that the Strain Theory, does not prove altogether true anymore, which stated that only lower classed people were the one's who had children misbehaving in schools. In schools which are public across the board of America behavior is a problem, and although class status comes into play these problems reach a multicultural educational system. Students in the class room show a multi level of problems, from personality disorder, to attention deficient disorder with emotional problems, and the teachers are expected through classroom management, to solve these issues. They are too big and too many to expect the educators to solve. It takes a "village to raise a child," as quoted by Hillary Clinton.

Students bring with them to the classroom problems of enormous magnitudes, that were once those of parents. How to feed a sibling, because the parent is on drugs and not there. Living in shelters and must come to school and be labeled by other's in the classroom. There surely must be an alternative program in place between the school system and the justice system to help these children change their behavior before they become the walking time bombs of the future. The children are crying out for love, for safety, for their basic need of psychological and emotional acceptance, yet no school system can provide all the need's in order to modify the behavior.

Case Studies

1. Little girl 12 years of age. She needs Ridlin medication, the mother can't afford it, and she doesn't get the medication. A typical day for the teacher, the child jumps up and down, disrupting the class, and yelling the whole class period, and she is on a 504b lesson plan, individualized work.

2. Little boy 13. His parents abandoned home, and he is in the court system, therefore he is angry and throws books, or hits other students. Detention does not solve his problem.

3. Little girl 12. Daydreams, sleeps, wakes up and starts yelling. Does no class work, home work, nothing. Molested by her step father.

4. Little girl has both parents. They work two jobs apiece, the child is at home by herself and tells the parents she has done all her home work and is a good student. The girl does not work and is disruptive, seeking attention the whole class period. The teacher calls parents, they don't understand.

There seems to be a bonding that is necessary from birth, and if the parents, grandparents and those who can don't give it, our schools and our communities will be a product of their environment. Behavior begins with each of us modeling for children, the things that are good, moral and just.

The Good Class

Ms. Curry is the new teacher, and this is her first day on the job. She is trying to teach Math and English, first by explaining multiplication and division, then subject and verbs in a sentence.

The students in her class are anxious to learn today as you can see.

Student #1 is so hard of hearing and her hearing aid is broken, so she constantly says, "What did you say? I can't hear you."

Student#2 is the smart one who knows all the answers and keeps her hand up in the air saying, "Let me answer! I know! I know!" and never gets called on.

Student # 3 cannot be still and keeps getting up and hitting other students. They keep saying, "Tell her to sit down."

Student# 4 is throwing paper every time Ms. Curry turns her back to write on the board. Ms. Curry asks, "What's going on? Who did that?" The whole class says, "Nothing Ms. Curry."

Student#5 is trying to explain the answer, but no one can understand what she says.

Eventually the class pays attention, and just before dismissal, Ms. Curry has them sing their slogan for today.

Sing-a-long

Slogan: I am gonna be somebody.

I got Science on my mind and Math in my hand.
(I'm gonna be somebody because I can) (Repeats three times.)

$E=mc^2$ you say,
I'm gonna be somebody because I can.
Old Einstein was back in the day.
I'm gonna be somebody because I can.
I know my History and you should too.
(I'm gonna be somebody because I can) (Repeats three times.)

Back to verse one, repeat.

Ends with Hey hey.

PART II

Education for the New Millennium

The child that has the ability to do well, and has not been encouraged by parents, teachers and others, that child becomes stagnated and lost in the system. Teachers have the responsibility to bring the love of learning from that child. To see that the student is not just another student, but an individual with potential. There are too many teachers who come to the classroom with stereotypes about certain students, either based on their past records and performances or the fact that the child was in a former teacher's class last year and gave her a hard time. This child already has a mental strike against them based on previous actions and reactions from another teacher. Educators have a responsibility to let go of all their faculty thinking and see each child in a positive light, no matter what the home situation. It does not matter whether the child has two parents in the home, or lives with foster parents. When that child is in that classroom the only things that the educator should consider are his or her ability to achieve greatness and instilling in students their ability to achieve greatness is the beginning of learning for most students. Students need to feel that you believe in them, that you expect them to succeed.

Too many teachers, are all about what school they graduated from, and what they know in their chosen field, as opposed to getting the information over to the students in a format that is easy for them to learn. No matter how difficult the subject matter, being able to present it in simple sequence steps is what makes learning fun and easy for the students and makes the difference. Not that I am saying to simplify the material so that it is on a much lower level, but making learning so that it's appropriate for the grade being taught, but easily understood. Education must change to fit the students, as opposed to being a standard that says all students must learn this or that. Every student will not learn the same way. Every student is not interested in the same subjects. Students should have the flexibility to change their curriculum, the flexibility to choose the courses that they are interested in and that they will do well in. Far too long people have worked in jobs that they hate, just to receive a pay check. It is time for this generation to work in fields that they want to work in and enjoy. If they are primarily interested in art, then schools need programs that structure their desire for that goal, as well as any other field. If a student wants to be a doctor, then from high school through college his courses should provide him with the knowledge that he needs for that field. It is time for education as a whole to change, to change not only to fit the average student, but the exceptional student as well, the gifted and advanced students as well as the exceptional student who is not so gifted.

There are jobs for everyone, and there are new ways of creating jobs. The student that is being left behind is not just the low achiever, but the one that is lost in the need to find a place in the work place after completing a college education. Education must not only tell how well you know math, science, English, government, history and the general studies, it should after 12-16 years of schooling present a well rounded individual who is well versed in all kinds of knowledge, and a person who knows who he is and what his goals are in life. There are too many people who have no idea what they want or where they are going, because not only has the school system failed them, but their parents may or may not have laid down a road map for them to follow. Everybody's parents were not college graduates with an idea of what they wanted before they got married and had children. We Have middle and high school students having babies before 21 and they are not prepared for the responsibilities of being parents, yet with all the birth control, there are more babies having babies today then there was in the 1960's.

For this generation to become the generation of future leaders for tomorrow, they must be qualified to compete with other students from other countries. They must be mentally and physically up to the challenge to compete in every area of education, whether it's the Olympics, or mental tests. Our students have become accustomed to just passing the end of term exams, or just passing the requirements for graduation. We would like to see students surpass any other nation, just because they are equipped to do and they can. Teachers should not feel the need to assist students in testing as a few have, because they should feel assured within themselves that the students are going to do well in what ever area they choose.

Education for the new millennium must also include retraining for the students who barely passed and graduated from high school, those who were socially promoted. Those who are in low paying jobs that require only a high school diploma, which seems in this day and age to serve little or no purpose other than to say that you completed your high school education. There are few jobs that require just a diploma, so for students who don't want to attend a four year college there must be something between the high school and the vocational technical school that prepares students to get the jobs that are skilled, technical and in demand. The ideal high school would do just that. It would prepare students who won't go to college for jobs, that will require a two year degree. When those students apply for these jobs, they would have been trained to go to work, whether it is as an automotive technician, an X-ray technician or any other skilled position.

Then there are the students who have the problems of addiction, who where born with the problems of addiction. Medication alone is not enough. These students have been labeled as special education or ADD or ADHD, and it will take skilled professionals to work with them and prepare them for the job market, but the school the only resource. Then the students who have behavior problems, they should have somewhere to go besides from schools to being incarcerated. This is normally due to low IQ and the problems of low socio economic status. If you look at the crime rates, the rates of poverty, there is a clear correlation between the two. The social services, the criminal justice department, all must work hand in hand to eliminate the problems. The schools have taken on too much. They cannot be parents, social workers, policeman and educators. It is time for parents to take control of their children and to make a consciousness effort to see that their children are on a course of action that will provide them with the best education possible, as a well rounded and well adjusted educated individual.

Another understated issue for the school system is knowing the background of the students. Teachers rarely have this information, and guidance counselors can only do so much. If the teachers are aware of the student's background, this will enable them to prevent some school shootings, not only to prevent bullying by students, but to nip it in the bud the moment it starts. Then there is the issue that keeps poking its ugly head of teachers getting out of college who are becoming involved with their students. This is unacceptable behavior and will not be tolerated. Any teacher certified by the state to teach should have a mental evaluation to determine if he or she, may be prone to be involved with a student. The idea is offensive, this borders on being a pedophile.

Educators are put into a position of trust, and once that trust is broken it not only sheds a dark light on one teacher, it makes all the teachers look bad. This is something that for all practical purposes should be eradicated.

Education must be varied. There should be schools that are just teaching math and science, schools that just teach engineering and schools that just teach nursing. Even charm schools need to come back, for the lack of manners and respect that we are seeing lately. In order for society to grow in a positive direction there must be change for the better, change that will allow the future generation to become more than they ever dreamed possible, with ability to make their dreams become a reality.

When a teacher sees a student walking down the hall with his pants falling down because they are two sizes too big and a bandana on, she or he has already formed an opinion of him before he steps foot in her class. It does not matter that he may be an A student, he may associate with a known criminal element, that child is already labeled as a potential trouble-maker or drop out. Each teacher is looking at his actions and grades, writing down everything possible against him, and even if he passes every class, when he applies to college they may not even recommend him. So what you look like, and how you present yourself is important, the same way that you would not go to a job interview with your jeans and T-shirt on if you want to get the job.

People never think about how they present themselves or that it really matters, but it does, and in some instances, there are some jobs that no matter how much you know you may need to know some one on the inside, but that is in low incidence. When you know that you know, what you know, no one can take the knowledge that you have acquired from your head, nor can they stop you from succeeding in the field that you choose once you apply yourself. The problem is getting the students to the point where they are accepted. The acceptance will more than likely start at an entry level position, yet most don't stay there long enough to move on. How many of us regret having left some job or another? Had we stayed, would we have been in a higher position with the years that passed? We have no way of knowing, yet we need to encourage our youth to start their own companies and to use their knowledge to become as great as they choose to be, without limitations. Some of us are stuck in jobs because that is all that there is. We stay there for 30 years without expecting or looking to move up or out. There are no limits to what anyone can become, so it is not our place to put limits on our students. Working towards their dreams, and becoming the top in their fields, will give them the courage to make a difference in the world as we know it today.

According, to the U.S supreme court decision of Brown Vs the Board of Education of 1954, it was decided that separate was not equal in education for African American students, yet today all groups attend the same classes and school in the public system, and they tend to segregate themselves into their own groups based on ethnicity.

There seems to be a variety of attitudes among the teachers, for or against some students, not in a racial or prejudice mode, but an air of indifference towards education of various students, as indicated by the research methods that examine the attitudes of teachers for educational change as done by the national research and development center and improving adult and school literacy. Which is included?

The Unites States Department of Education under the No Child Left Behind act will be requiring all states to comply in meeting the challenge of high school students being required to complete three courses in Science and three in Math to graduate.

The problem with that is that, prior to students getting to high school these students have little knowledge if any of science. Understandably, this is necessary in order for students to prepare to compete in a global market, but this needs to start at the elementary and middle school level first. There also needs to be in place a program that does not require this, for the special education or the handicapped student, understanding all inclusive education, but these students are required to take the same tests as others and it is not fair if they are not mentally capable due to an illness.

It seems to me that all the students are being lumped together by age, group and class with the expectation to complete the same thing, that in itself is not possible with students on different grade levels within the same class, as well as IEP's. No Child Left Behind will leave more students in the higher grades behind, before it will benefit them.

Research References

Deconstructing The At Risk Student, by John Agada

U.S. Department of Education: *Meeting the Challenge of A Challenging World*

We Shall Overcome, Brown Vs Board of Education

We Shall Overcome, John P. Sousa School

Quantitative & Qualitative Research Methods to determine the Attitudes of Teachers, www.nrdc.org

Curriculum, by John D. Me Neil

Therapist Guide, by Sharon L. Johnson

The Power of the Subconscious Mind, by Joseph Murphy PhD

Actual case studies from various schools.

Educational Foundations and Human Growth and Development / Effective Teacher Training, by Open Court Publishing & McGraw-Hill books.

www.ingramcontent.com/pod-product-compliance
Lightning Source LLC
Chambersburg PA
CBHW030542290526
45786CB00004B/1821